D1611909

Born to be Wild
Little Penguins

Anne Jonas

Words that appear in the glossary are printed in
boldface type the first time they occur in the text.

Gareth Stevens
Publishing

Snug and Warm

Crack! Crack! A baby emperor penguin hatches from its egg, just like thousands of other penguin chicks on the **ice floe**. Its father watches closely. He has been **incubating** the egg, or keeping it warm with his body, for about two months. He has not moved away from the egg — not even for a second. Where is the little penguin's mother? After laying the egg, she went to find food in the sea. Now, after the chick is born, its mother comes back. Then, its father will go off to find food.

Although penguins are seabirds, emperor penguins are born very far from the sea. A young emperor penguin will not make its first dive into the cold waters that surround Antarctica for several months.

What do you think?

Why does a penguin chick snuggle between its father's or mother's legs after it is born?

a) because it is scared

b) because it does not know how to walk

c) because sitting on ice is too cold

3

Emperor penguins are born in the coldest place on Earth. On the ice floes where they live, the temperature can be as cold as −58° Fahrenheit (−50° Celsius) — much colder than in a food freezer!

A little penguin stays warm between the legs of one of its parents until it becomes stronger and grows a warm layer of **down**. From time to time, however, the chick sticks its head out of its cozy shelter to look at the huge area of ice and snow around it.

Little penguins do not have adult feathers. They are covered only with fuzzy gray down.

4

A penguin often leans backward and rests on its heels and its tail so the tips of its toes will not freeze.

When it becomes an adult, a penguin is well-protected from the cold by a thick layer of fat and very tight, waterproof feathers.

In nice weather, especially while they **brood**, penguins turn their black backs toward the Sun to help hold in heat.

Mother Is Home

When a mother penguin comes back from the sea, she looks for her **mate** and meets her chick for the first time. Her trip to find food was long because penguins lay their eggs about 65 miles (105 kilometers) from the sea. People can travel that distance in about one hour by car, but penguins must walk for about one month to go this far. Penguins have very short legs, and although they have wings, they cannot fly.

What do you think?

How does a female penguin recognize her mate when she comes back from the sea?

a) by his singing

b) by his feathers

c) by the way he **waddles**

Penguins gather together in a group, or **colony**, called a **rookery** to lay eggs and raise chicks. Thousands of penguins live in the same rookery.

A female penguin has trouble finding her mate in a crowd of several thousand penguins. The only way she can find him is to wander around the colony singing and wait for him to sing back. Because no two penguins sing the same way, a pair of penguins can recognize each other's voices.

A female penguin recognizes her mate by his singing.

When she returns from the sea, a female penguin brings up to 7 pounds (3 kilograms) of fish and shrimp with her. She carries them in a kind of pouch that is located between her mouth and her stomach.

To feed his chick until its mother returns with food, a father penguin **regurgitates** a cereal-like substance and slides it into the chick's beak.

A penguin family's reunion does not last long. As soon as the female returns, the male leaves for the sea. He has not eaten anything except snow for about four months!

9

Everybody to the Nursery

By the time penguin chicks are six weeks old, they have already grown a lot, and the down covering their bodies has become very thick. They can now leave their snug shelters between their mothers' or fathers' legs and walk on the frozen ground. In only a few days, their parents will leave for the seashore. While their mothers and fathers are away, the chicks stay gathered together in a kind of nursery, where a few other adult penguins watch over them.

These little penguins are waiting for their parents to return. The chicks will recognize their parents' singing and answer by singing back.

Why do penguins form colonies so far from the sea?

a) because they want to escape the wind

b) because they are afraid the chicks will fall into the water

c) because they love long trips

Penguins form their colonies so far from the sea to escape the wind.

Even though the wind **inland** is not as strong as at the seashore, it can still reach speeds of up to 135 miles (217 km) per hour.

During storms, strong blasts of wind can turn ice crystals into millions of tiny flying needles. To protect themselves, penguins snuggle against each other.

Penguins' very short legs make walking difficult, so a trip to the sea is a long journey

Penguins move from place to place by waddling on their webbed feet. They walk a little like people might walk if their pants slid down around their ankles.

Penguins love tobogganing. They slide down slopes on their big round bellies, using their paws to push themselves forward. Sliding is much easier than walking!

An ice floe is very slippery. Fortunately, a penguin's feet have strong claws to keep the bird from falling.

The Big Dive

When a young penguin is old enough and strong enough, it travels to the sea for the first time. The penguin makes this journey with its parents. At the sea, it will be able to play in the waves and feast on fish and shrimp. On its first big dive, a young penguin **instinctively** knows how to swim and how to feed itself.

What do you think?

What does a penguin do before diving?

a) It fluffs its feathers.

b) It carefully looks at the water to see if dangerous animals are nearby.

c) It tests the temperature of the water with its toes.

When a little penguin is five months old, its body will lose its fluffy down and become covered with waterproof feathers. The penguin needs these new feathers to stay warm when it swims in cold water.

Before diving, a penguin carefully looks at the water to see if any dangerous animals are swimming nearby.

Penguins may be slow and clumsy on the ground, but they are fast and graceful in the water. Even though their swimming skills are very good, they must watch out for sea lions and killer whales. Sea lions and killer whales eat penguins! When a penguin is in danger, it swims to shore as fast as it can. As it swims, the penguin constantly changes direction to confuse its attacker.

When they dive, penguins belly flop into the water, then swim deep beneath the surface.

Like dolphins, penguins can leap over waves. By leaping while they swim, penguins can move even faster and do not become as tired. To come out of the water, penguins **propel** themselves onto the ice.

When they hunt, penguins chose their **prey** and then chase it. Penguins eat shrimp, small fish, and squid, catching them with their powerful beaks.

Penguins are excellent divers, able to chase their prey as deep as 900 feet (275 meters). Penguins can stay underwater without breathing for up to about twenty minutes.

All Ashore

After two months of swimming and stuffing themselves with fish, all the penguins come back on shore. The youngest penguins, which are now adults, return to their birthplaces. The time has come for them to start laying eggs and raising chicks. When the penguins reach their **destinations**, the females wander around their colonies to find mates. To attract a female, a male penguin sings and bows as it waddles. Most female penguins will each lay two eggs, but female emperor penguins will each lay only one egg. The male emperors then will brood, or sit on and hatch the egg.

During a long trip across an ice floe, a colony of penguins always chooses the shortest way to travel and never gets lost.

What do you think?

What do penguins do to stay warm while they brood?

a) They build cozy nests.

b) They shake their wings.

c) They huddle together.

To stay warm while they brood, penguins huddle together.

A brooding male cannot uncover its egg for one second or the egg will freeze immediately. To stay warm while they brood, male penguins huddle together. The penguins in the center of the huddle regularly trade places with the penguins on the outside of the huddle so they all can take their turns warming up. Any materials that penguins might use to build a warm, cozy nest are impossible to find on an ice floe.

As soon as a male penguin receives an egg, he covers it with a thick fold of skin, called a brood pouch, which is located at the bottom of his stomach. The temperature under this feathery covering can be almost 90°F (32°C).

After a female penguin lays an egg, she carefully slides it onto her mate's feet so the egg will not touch the frozen ground.

During their two months of brooding, male penguins lose up to half their body weight.

21

Penguins are birds, which means their bodies are covered with feathers, and they each have a beak and wings. Penguins cannot fly, but they are excellent swimmers. They live in the southern half of the world, in areas surrounded by freezing cold oceans. Emperor penguins live only along the edges of Antarctica. They can live up to forty years in the wild. An adult emperor penguin weighs between about 50 and 85 pounds (23 and 38 kg). The penguin family includes seventeen kinds of penguins. King penguins look similar to emperor penguins, but they are smaller in size, have longer beaks, and have orange feathers on their upper breasts.

Penguins cannot fly. Over time, their wings became stiff, flat flippers.

Emperor penguins are the world's largest penguins. From head to toe, an emperor penguin is nearly 48 inches (122 centimeters) tall — about the size of a seven-year-old child.

A penguin often uses its short tail as a third foot.

An emperor penguin's beak is black with an orange stripe on each side. A penguin has a very rough tongue, which helps it catch slippery prey, such as fish.

Some kinds of penguins have yellowish orange spots on the sides of their necks.

Every adult penguin has a coat of waterproof feathers that is black on the back and white in front.

A penguin's feet have powerful claws that keep the bird from slipping and sliding on ice.

23

GLOSSARY

Antarctica — the cold, icy land that surrounds the South Pole

brood — (v) to sit on and hatch eggs

colony — a group of one kind of animal living together

destinations — the end points of trips or journeys

down — fine, soft, fluffy feathers

ice floe — a large, flat area of ice floating in a body of water

incubating — providing warmth to an egg so the chick growing inside can develop and hatch

inland — the part of a body of land that is far from the sea

instinctively — naturally, without having to be taught

mate — (n) the male or female of a pair of animals

prey — animals that are hunted and killed by other animals

propel — to move forward with a forceful motion

regurgitates — brings food back up into the mouth after it has been chewed and swallowed

rookery — a colony or breeding ground for large numbers of birds and some mammals, such as penguins and seals

seabirds — birds that spend a lot of time on the open ocean

waddles — walks with short steps, swaying the body from side to side

Please visit our web site at: **www.garethstevens.com**
For a free color catalog describing Gareth Stevens Publishing's list of high-quality books and multimedia programs, call **1-800-542-2595 (USA) or 1-800-387-3178 (Canada).**
Gareth Stevens Publishing's fax: 1-877-542-2596

Library of Congress Cataloging-in-Publication Data

Jonas, Anne.
  [Petit manchot. English]
  Little penguins / Anne Jonas. — North American ed.
    p. cm. — (Born to be wild)
  ISBN 0-8368-4738-5 (lib. bdg.)
  1. Penguins—Infancy—Juvenile literature. I. Title. II. Series.
QL696.S473J6513 2005
598.47'139—dc22   2004065365

This North American edition first published in 2006 by
Gareth Stevens Publishing
A Weekly Reader Company
1 Reader's Digest Rd.
Pleasantville, NY 10570-7000 USA

This U.S. edition copyright © 2006 by Gareth Stevens, Inc.
Original edition copyright © 2001 by Mango Jeunesse.

First published in 2001 as *Le petit manchot* by Mango Jeunesse, an imprint of Editions Mango, Paris, France.

Picture Credits (t = top, b = bottom, l = left, r = right)
Bios: R. Philips 5(tl); A. Torterotot cover, 5(bl), 20, 22; D. Cox 12, 15; V. Cox, P. Arnold back cover; R. Schoen 13(r); Seitre 16; T. Thierry 21(b). PHONE: Y. Husianycia title page, 2, 18; G. Robertson 3, 7, 13(tl, b), 17(t), 21(t); J. P. Ferrero 5(r). Jacana: W. Wisniewski 8(l); F. Polking 11. Sunset: E. Pott 4; West Stock 6; FLPA 9, 10; ANT 8(r); Animals Animals 17(bl, r); Alaska Stock 22–23.

English translation: Muriel Castille
Gareth Stevens editor: Barbara Kiely Miller
Gareth Stevens art direction: Tammy West

Printed in the United States of America

2 3 4 5 6 7 8 9 10 09 08